Read this book with a heart that yearns to hear the concerns that are foremost in Christ's heart as He looks upon the church in this hour. Bob shares many gentle prophetic challenges, made urgent through the prophetic dreams he's received. This book will surprise you in the way it will suddenly pierce your heart. Let's respond to Bob's prophetic call—let's become intercessory watchmen on the wall until we see the city transformation our Lord has promised.

Bob Sorge, author, www.oasishouse.net

The Call to the Wall is a prophetic insight into our generation, and the call of God to us to be a people who tirelessly and importunately ask God in prayer and intercession to rend the heavens and come down and do things we do not expect. Bob Hartley is a faithful intercessor. His prophetic thrust and voice has matured in the House of Prayer over the past 22 years. If there be a prophet in the land let him intercede. This is true of Bob Hartley. I have enjoyed reading The Call to the Wall and highly recommend a prayerful reading of this prophetic challenge.

Noel Alexander, President, Love Mercy, www.lovemercy.com

This is a very important book for you to read if you want to be an effective intercessor. It is a journey to discover God's heart and will so your prayers hit the mark. The depth of revelation and understanding God has given my friend, Bob Hartley, is compelling and unique. It is a fresh prophetic trumpet sound to summon the battle-weary saints to the wall again! Call to the Wall is a "now" word to the body of Christ for the serious times we live in. It is replete with scriptures and keys to walk and pray in this critical hour. Bob shares dreams and visions the Lord has given him, which will give you language and understanding for your journey into the heart of Jesus, The Intercessor!

Jill Austin, President & Founder, Master Potter Ministries, author and conference speaker, www.masterpotter.com.

The art of discerning the times and the seasons is being restored in this critical hour. One of those voices that is being raised up in this hour is my friend of years Bob (Robert if it needs to be) Hartley. The message and the messenger have become one. A Call to the Wall is prophetic, piercing and timely. Read, weep, and then take a big, deep breath of the empowering grace of God and mount yourself on the walls of intercession for such a time as this.

Dr. James (Jim) W. Goll, Encounters Network, author

I have known Bob Hartley for years and immensely look up to him in the place of calling marketplace people to the wall of intercession. He is an example to the next generation of business people building on their knees in prayer and calling cities forth into their mission and purpose in God's sight. We're fully joining our hearts with this purpose of marketplace people being called to the wall of intercession and prayer.

Dwayne Roberts, Director of Onething Ministries at the International House of Prayer in Kansas City, www.onethingglobal.com.

Divinely inspired dreams have a unique way of bringing spiritual truths into our hearts from new angles. The word pictures and word plays embedded within them, when rightly decoded, seem to make the ancient Biblical teachings and commands they reflect come alive, penetrate the defenses around our souls and be imprinted on our minds and emotions.

Divine dreams mysteriously can motivate us to reconnect with God and serve Him with greater fervor. For many years, God has periodically visited Bob Hartley through the gift of dreams. I have been impacted by the Holy Spirit on more than one occasion by dreams that Bob has specifically received from God for my benefit. The dreams and their applications that Bob reports to us in this little book have served to expand his heart in a wonderful way and, by this and many other means, he has become a man with a truly great heart for both God and people. May our God use these simply profound and profoundly simple pictures and parables -- God's "sign-language" -- to likewise expand our hearts, the hearts of many other followers of Jesus Christ and even the hearts of those yet to be born.

Psalm 78:2-4
2 I will open my mouth in a parable;
   I will utter dark sayings of old,
3 Which we have heard and known,
   And our fathers have told us.
4 We will not hide them from their children,
   Telling to the generation to come the praises of the LORD,
   And His strength and His wonderful works that He has
done.

Michael Sullivant, pastor, author and teacher, Kansas City 2006

THE CALL TO THE WALL

a prophetic decree

BY ROBERT HARTLEY

The Call the the Wall

Published by:

> New Grid Publishing
> 11184 Antioch #354
> Overland Park, KS 66210

For additional copies, visit www.newgridbooks.com.

Edited by Robert Fraser and Pippa Kendall. Cover design by Shawn Blanc.

International Standard Book Number: 0–9753905–2–X

dedication

This book is dedicated to four special people who have been instrumental in the formation of these messages in my heart.

Firstly, to Bob Jones, who is a life-long prophetic mentor and friend. He challenged me to discover God not only in the "corner of church" but also in cities and all walks of life. He has dreamed with me of cities being restored to God. He has loved me well as a friend and as a divine perspective-changer.

Secondly, to Mike Bickle, with whom I have walked since 1983 and who has been such a friend to me and my family. Mike was the key to the opening up of the reality of "building on my knees." As his youth pastor from 1983 to 1991 he made it my job description to study God's promises and pray them. Most of all his stirring love for Jesus and his discovery of Him has gripped me deeply. I am "called to the wall" by his very life.

Thirdly, to Bob Fraser, who has blazed the trail as a pioneer in the discovery of God in the marketplace and in cities. He has been a best friend, committed with me to call marketplace people to the wall and spend our lives together in this.

Finally, and most of all, to Terry Hartley, my wife. She is the most remarkable person I know. She lives "on the wall." Her example is unparalleled and astounding, and seeing the results of her prayer gives me confidence in this place of the Call to the Wall.

contents

foreword

In Daniel 9:1, Daniel realized that the 70 years of exile proscribed by Jeremiah was complete. Daniel could have done many good things: he could have approached the king, or organized a reconstruction committee. Instead, Daniel turned first to God, seeking God in prayer and fasting for 21 days. Daniel understood that an answer from the throne of God was the first answer he should seek.

At the end of his fast, the angel Gabriel appeared to Daniel and stated in verse 23, "At the beginning of your supplications the command was issued, and I have come to tell you." When Daniel prayed and fasted, heavenly commands were issued, and angels responded. While other dimensions of human activity are often good and necessary, prayer and fasting is indispensable. *Prayer and fasting is the only way for humans to obtain heavenly decrees and move angels and demons.*

In 1983 God spoke to us supernaturally that we were to begin "24/7 prayer in the spirit of the Tabernacle of David." We didn't have much understanding of this directive, but as a church we began un-anointed, poorly-attended prayer meetings four times per day. Then in 1999, some 16 years later, I was freshly charged by God to pursue this mandate. I resigned as pastor of the church and started, in a small trailer (bought for us by Bob Hartley!), the International House of Prayer in Kansas City, (IHOP-KC) a 24/7 prayer room modeled on the Tabernacle of David.

Since that time, God has performed miracle upon miracle and poured out His grace again and again, to help us stand firm in our purpose and nurture our growth. Because of this power and grace, that prayer meeting has never stopped, and today there are several hundred full-time intercessors together going "hard" after this purpose, and thousands more involved with us in some way.

IHOP-KC is but a tiny part of the global prayer movement being awakened today by the hand of God. Prayer rooms of all sorts are popping up in cities worldwide. Hardly a day goes by when I do not hear of a new citywide house of prayer, or a Church-based house of prayer (Church HOP) or a business-based house of prayer (BizHOP) starting. Peter Grieg's 24/7 prayer movement is a global phenomenon. The largest prayer meeting in history, the "Global Day of Prayer," took place on June 4, 2006 with prayer meetings in 198 nations and between 400 and 500 million believers. Interest in prayer amongst the body of Christ worldwide has never been higher. Though we are only at the beginning of the beginning, God is clearly on the move.

What is God up to? Why is He stirring up this prayer movement? There are many, many reasons, but here is a central one.

God is awakening love and wholeheartedness in His people. Wholehearted means our heart is "whole" – not divided between Him and anything else. David expressed it like this: "One thing I desire, that I shall seek, that I may dwell in the house of the Lord all the days of my life" (Ps. 27:4). He has held nothing back in His love for us, and His greatest desire is for a people whose love for Him is equally unhindered in return – a suitable, equally-yoked, single-eyed, passionate, love-struck bride for His Son.

From the beginning, this was His desire – intimate fellowship with man, and the giving and receiving of voluntary love with us. The Garden of Eden was created for intimate fellowship (Gen 3:8). The first and greatest commandment (Dt. 6:5, Mt. 22:36) is to love our God with all our heart, soul, mind and strength. What God is really after couldn't be clearer: the wholehearted, voluntary love of human beings.

Jesus reaffirmed the Father's primary aim of love and intimate fellowship with man. *He defined the cross as an act of friendship and love* (John 15:13). In demonstrating such magnanimous love, and making such an extraordinary offer of friendship to all, Jesus not only affirmed the Father's desire, but also empowered the human heart to respond. His demonstration of extraordinary love for us ignites the hearts of weak and inwardly torn human beings like me, empowering our hearts to press in:

> [14]For the love of Christ controls [compels, perplexes, preoccupies] us, having concluded this, that one died for all, therefore all died. 2 Cor. 5:14 (NASB)

> [1]Therefore I urge you, brethren, [in view of the compassions] of God, to present your bodies a living and holy sacrifice, acceptable to God, which is your spiritual service of worship. Rom. 12:1

> [20]"I have been crucified with Christ; and it is no longer I who live, but Christ lives in me; and the life which I now live in the flesh I live by faith in the Son of God, *who loved me* and gave Himself up for me. Gal 2:20 (NASB)

In John 17:26 Jesus prayed a prophetic prayer. In this prayer He articulates where He is taking His church. He asked that the love that the Father has for the Son would be in His people also. Here is what this means: before human history is concluded, *the same love the Father has for Jesus will be fully manifested in His people*. God will have a people so completely and fully in love with Jesus, it will be called *the same* as the Father's love for Jesus. *Amazing!*

As we approach the climax of human history, all things are being summed into the Son (Eph. 1:10). Prior to this final day, the earth will experience increasing turmoil and difficulty, reaching culmination in the Great Tribulation, a time of unprecedented pressure on the planet. God's purpose is not destruction or punishment, but to remove everything from our lives that hinders this abandoned love for the Son of God. Most believers have things in their lives that hinder abandoned love: money, security, relationships, earthly success, etc. These "props" will be increasingly challenged, forcing us to choose what we really love. For those who really don't want to love Him, He will give them ample reason to reject Him and rage against Him. For those who really want to love Him, He will show Himself to be everything they ever desired and needed, and more. Their love will grow stronger and more passionate. So evil will become more evil, and righteousness will become more righteous.

This final "day of the Lord" was foreshadowed in the cataclysmic events of 605BC when Nebuchadnezzar conquered Jerusalem. 15-20 years prior to this invasion, the prophet Joel prophesied and wrote the Book of Joel. This book is prophetic for our day. It beautifully answers the questions of what we are to do prior to difficulty and pressure, and how we are to respond in the midst of it.

In this prophetic book, God clearly articulates what He is looking for from His people:

> [12] "Return to Me with all your heart, and with fasting, weeping and mourning;
> [13] And rend your heart and not your garments." Now return to the LORD your God, For He is gracious and compassionate, Slow to anger, abounding in lovingkindness.
> Joel 2:12-13 (NASB).

Joel goes on to give clear instruction:

> [15] Blow a trumpet in Zion,
> Consecrate a fast, proclaim a solemn assembly,
> [16] Gather the people, sanctify the congregation,
> Assemble the elders,
> Gather the children and the nursing infants
> Joel 2:15-16 (NASB)

God is calling His people to wholeheartedness – and prayer and fasting are God's methodology to produce wholeheartedness in human beings. God is calling His people to prayer and fasting through many various means and expressions, such as the "Call to the Wall."

The "Call to the Wall" is a powerful call straight from the heart of God to all believers about the times and seasons we are in, and the strategies and purposes of God in these days. I highly recommend this book as a glimpse into the heart of God and His purposes for us in the Body of Christ.

I have walked with Bob as a friend for over 20 years, and not only do I commend to you the message of this book, but I also commend to you Bob as a true brother in Christ and a profound prophetic voice to the Body of Christ.

Mike Bickle,

July 2006, Kansas City

CHAPTER ONE

ask again

I had a dream in early 2005 where I was crying out with others for the saints. I saw that in their current state they were weak and beaten up due to a lack of perceived help. I so felt for the saints, it seemed like they had endured so much. Isaiah 42:3 says, "A bruised reed he will not break, and a smoldering wick he will not snuff out. In faithfulness he will bring forth justice."

A Plaintive Cry

I saw that we had a "plaintive" cry to God, mournful and pitiable. The Lord responded to this plaintive cry, He said, "Help is on its way;" but then he said the real issue is "Why don't you trust me? Aren't I a friend? Don't friends trust friends? I am not the incompetent God; I have been there for you and you have not perceived me. You have strange memories; you always remember the rejection rather than my leading love. You need a new view, rather than viewing everything through the filter of rejection. All you have to do is ask me again, from a place of trust. Just keep asking again."

He continued, "Many have asked once, twice, even three times, but quickly come to the end of their own strength in asking when they don't really trust me. Ask again with a different attitude – the Mahalalel attitude."

The "Mahalalel" Attitude

A few years back when I was studying the scriptures, God led me to the Noahic genealogy in Genesis 5, and I saw the ways of God with his people unfold in the names from one generation to the next.

This name, "Mahalalel," from the Noahic genealogy, means "but the blessed God," or "the praise of God." This name reflects the attitude that knows that God has the trump card in any situation. Though it may seem like the enemy has laid down four aces, but God wants us to understand and believe that He can change everything in an instant – he has the power to trump every circumstance and every situation.

The Great Provoker

In the dream the scene moved to 1 Kings 18:33–35. Elijah was outnumbered 800 to one. The land was ruled by evil. Circumstances looked bleak. But Elijah was unmoved, and in the test of fire against the prophets of Baal, he poured water on the altar and then more water on the altar before calling fire down from heaven. Elijah understood that nothing was too difficult for God.

The Lord was speaking through this example that although for a season our circumstances may appear to grow worse (like more water being poured on the altar), it's really just an opportunity to obtain a new view of "the God who is able," where harder circumstances are simply an opportunity for a greater victory and greater glory to God.

Jesus is visiting us as the "Great Provoker" to bring greater pressure upon us, but then to meet us in it. God is allowing the present difficult circumstances to move us to ask again. And in the asking again for His view, we gain a key revelation and a true prize: an expanded understanding of God.

In contrast, many modern-day believers respond to difficult circumstances by seeing it as rejection. It's all about right perspective – we must get this new view, God's altogether different view, that circumstances might be tough, "but the blessed God" has all the trump cards!

I believe this is God's challenge and exhortation to us – in the dream he asked, "When are you going to get the best view that comes from me? When are you going to see things the way I see things?"

Dusting Ourselves Off

Over many I saw demonic spirits that had been assigned to misinterpret every circumstance, lie against the character of God, and sow dissatisfaction into the hearts of believers. I was astonished at the level of success they had had – many complacently accepted every evil thought that was suggested to them. I was even more astonished to see that this place of plaintive, defeated drudgery had become a place they had actually become comfortable in.

Many have been deeply tested by tragedies and difficult circumstances, and have grown battle-weary. But Hebrews 12:3 exhorts us, "Consider him (Jesus) who endured such opposition...so that you will not grow weary and lose heart." Many have not considered Him, and have grown weary and lost heart.

We have allowed these tests to weigh on our soul, and we have lost some of our ability to trust in God. We have become like Zechariah, the father of John the Baptist. When an angel appeared to Zechariah and foretold the wondrous birth of John the Baptist, he could not believe, but could only question: "How can I be sure of this?" (Luke 1:18). Zechariah had lost his "faith reach" in God. There are many like that today who have allowed life to take its toll, and have stopped believing for the promises of God, retreating into a personal mission of earthly success.

Many have not processed their seasons of testing well. At one point, Jesus asked us, "Why do you turn every difficult circumstance into a question of my love?" We have asked the wrong questions, turning every circumstance into a question of His love, or a question of our failure, rather than understanding it as the bible commands: as training for our good (Heb 12:4-11). We must learn not to ask illegal questions that damage our faith and cause us to sin in unbelief like Zechariah – questions like, "How could God allow this?" Or, "What have I done to deserve this?" We must inquire of God for His heart and insight, and ask the right questions, like: "God, what are you doing through this?" "How am I to respond?" "How am I to see you in this?"

God is saying it is time for the promises to be fulfilled, but we must begin to believe once more and ask again. It is time to dust off our old promises, hopes and dreams and begin to believe them freshly, and ask with a new confidence, attitude and view in Him.

A Confident Proclamation

The story of Habbakuk is like a prayer journal of the transition from a plaintive cry to a confident proclamation of His promises. Our current cry is like Habbakuk 1:1: "How long, O Lord, must I call for help, but you do not listen? Or cry out to you 'Violence!' but you do not save?"

But by the end of the book, Habbakuk had obtained the "Mahalalel" attitude of confidence in God: "

> [17]Though the fig tree does not bud and there are no grapes on the vines, though the olive crop fails and the fields produce no food, though there are no sheep in the pen and no cattle in the stalls, [18]yet I will rejoice in the Lord, I will be joyful in God my Savior. [19]The Sovereign Lord is my strength, he makes my feet like the feet of a deer, he enables me to go on the heights." Habbakuk 3:17-19

He wants to enable us to "go on the heights" where we can see from His viewpoint – above the "clouds" of our doubt and perplexity. This is the current invitation for modern-day saints, to move to the new view, God's overcoming view, like Habbakuk. This new view will cause us to ask and ask again, with trust and faith. It is even OK if we start with a plaintive cry so long as we begin asking again, and we ask knowing that God has a trump card, and that he can be trusted. We are one step away from entering into a place where we see life from a whole different perspective.

Utterly Amazed

I saw that when we got this new view, Habbakuk 1:5 would begin to happen: "Look at the nations and watch – and be utterly amazed. For I am going to do something in your days that you would not believe even if you were told." I saw God coming to surprise us with swift and astonishing answers far beyond our wildest imagination. God is going to move in such ways that sets our hearts ablaze in love for Him and His promises and sets our faith on a whole new level.

CHAPTER TWO

sons of jacob

Attaining the Summit

God is inviting His people to move into a wholly different view of life. He wants to show us what He sees; He wants us to see His leading love throughout all the circumstances of our lives. He wants to clear the fog of our unbelief that perceives rejection rather than his leading love.

He is going to give a gift to those of us who want to receive it: He will take us to the "summit," a high hill of His perspective, to see His heart and His promises over our lives, our cities, and our nations. He is asking us, "When are you going to allow me to give you the best view of life?"

Sons of Jacob

I recently had a dream in which God showed me that he wants modern-day saints to become "Sons of Jacob" – those who wrestle in prayer with vigor and earnestness, those who ask "hard" for the promises of God, who see his leading love and who do not give up. Throughout scripture (Ps 44, Ps 84) the term "Sons of Jacob" is used to signify those who are tenacious in their pursuit of the promises of God.

Jacob wrestled for his promises and his inheritance, even when death stood before him. He kept asking and wrestling, and this *pleased God.* "Your name will no longer be Jacob, but Israel (meaning 'he struggles with God'), because you have struggled with God and with men and have overcome." (Gen 32:28). Many saints do not wrestle for their promises, but say in their hearts, "If God wants me to have it, then He will give it to me." This attitude may appear like humility, but it is not. God is pleased when we wrestle for the promises God has given.

In the dream, the Lord had a complaint over us: that we had too easily given up on faith rather than fighting for our promises like Jacob. Our cries had become weak and plaintive. We had allowed our faith and confidence to die. God said, "They view life thinking I'm really rejecting them and that I'm deaf to their cries."

God is asking us to move from a plaintive, mournful cry to a Jacob wrestling – one that is confident in Him and his leading love, and one that is not ashamed to wrestle for that which God has given.

The Privilege of Co-laboring

The kind of wrestling God is inviting us into is a co–laboring with Him and his heart's desires to bring about his purposes on the earth – an awesome privilege.

God's promises have been released into the heavens but we must ask for these to be loosed on earth – Ps 115:16, "The highest heavens belong to the Lord, but the earth he has given to man." When God gave man a free will, He gave us both the dignity and privilege of asking for "the kingdom to come on earth as it is in heaven" (Matthew 6:10).

Underestimating a Third Party

In my dream we had underestimated the hindering presence of a third party – the devil. The devil does not want these promises loosed on earth and wars violently against them.

We have to wrestle against the enemy, through unrelenting prayer and belief, for these promises to be loosed on earth. It is a noble fight to co–labor with God. But without this intercession He doesn't have permission to move – we effectively and tragically "dis–invite God" from moving in the earth.

Our Three Sins

In the dream, there were 3 sins that prevented us taking our place as the Sons of Jacob.

The first sin was the sin of shame. We had a shame like the prodigal son in Luke 15, seeing only our own weakness and failure. We had returned to the Father but believed we had really blown it. We were hoping only for a life of hard work, to beg for a measly job like the prodigal son did. He had no faith to ask the Father for anything more.

In the dream God said we were in the same place. Regarding our weakness and failure, He said, "You are actually far worse than what you think – *but you are far, far more loved than what you think*." We do not realize the depth of the love of our Father, who will run after us and reward us in spite of our shortcomings and shame. God wants us to experience this, just as the prodigal did.

God said, "The hardest thing required of you that you'll ever have to do is believe for my love, believe for my inheritance all the days of your life. It's my joy to invite you fully into my heart and my promises. I'm going to do this because I take pleasure in my people. Oh that you would know me, understand me and rejoice in your Maker!"

Second, we had the sin of foolish naivety. We had underestimated the presence of a third party – the presence of the enemy. The picture he gave me was like the foolish man in Proverbs 7:6-27. This man was naively sauntering down the street and walked right into the trap laid for him by a sly and cunning harlot. He was unprepared for the challenge and as a result was totally outmatched and easily overcome by the ancient and wily enemy.

In the dream he said we were in the place of Isaiah 56. Many have made sincere efforts to pray and pursue God and have gained a measure of the joy of knowing God and his wonderful purpose for their lives. They got the initial promise and ran out joyfully to build. But they had not adequately considered that they might be strongly opposed by the enemy. They were naively unprepared for the traps laid for them by the cunning enemy and were completely outmatched. They experienced the "pioneer fade" when their promises got challenged and they experienced the first bit of opposition. Then the third party, the "beasts of the field" of Is 56:9 came in and devoured them. Then they became like Is 56:10 – blind to the promises, blind to the knowledge of God.

It's a double robbery – the enemy steals the saints' inheritance and then blames God! They think God is opposing them, rather than the "beasts of the field" – the third party.

Third, the sin of self–reliance crept in. Out of disappointment and our wrong view of God we had become like the Israelites in Haggai 1. Haggai 1:2-3 says, "This is what the Lord Almighty says: "These people say, 'The time has not yet come for the lord's house to be built.' Then the word of the Lord came to Haggai: 'Is it a time for you yourselves to be living in your paneled houses, while this house remains a ruin?'" We were no longer reaching for the promises of God and His purposes, but we were content just to build our own houses in our own strength, focusing on prospering our own lives. It was a pitiful, diminished perspective, missing the far better invitation to build God's house – a "house of prayer for all nations."

In the dream, God was not angry at us, but passionate for us. He wanted us to stop killing ourselves vainly and stupidly building our own empires, our own paneled houses – he could see how it was exhausting and diminishing us, stealing our true eternal inheritance. To co-labor with Him and his heart was so much better, where there are endless resources, grace and power, and a far better reward.

Our real work is to learn to lean on Him. Song 8:6: "Who is this coming up from the desert, leaning on her beloved?"

The Promise: A New Heart

The promise was that if we would repent of our self reliant, plaintive position and move to the place of asking from a new view, wrestling as co–laborers, as Sons of Jacob then he would give us new hearts: His very heart. I saw God would thrust his hand into our chests and

touch our hearts. We were gripped in the deepest places of our soul –
we were changed and given an incurable desire for his desires.

In the dream, God was inviting us into a lifetime of partnering with
Him through asking for and releasing His promises in prayer. God
was so blessed when we asked Him and trusted in Him from the
place of this new heart, that felt His heart.

CHAPTER THREE

going to the garden

Many years ago the Lord called me "to the wall" – the Isaiah 62:6 call: "I have posted watchmen on your walls, O Jerusalem; they will never be silent day or night. You who call on the Lord give yourselves no rest." I said "yes" to the call, expecting the groaning and wailing of intercession; but what actually happened first was that the Lord began to show me His heart and what He cared for.

Finding His Heart

To my surprise, when He called me to prayer, He first took me on a journey of discovering His heart for me, for others and for Himself. I believe that it's to be the same journey for many of us.

I had a series of dreams in which the Lord asked me questions: "How do you feel about your wife? Or about your children? How did your father feel about you?" I remember responding with exhilarated joy to these questions – that I so loved my wife, everything about her, and that I'd be nothing without her; that my children were my absolute delight, each one unique and special to my heart in so many ways; and that my father loved me constantly, even when I was difficult, dealing drugs in the past – it didn't change a thing in his love for me.

Then the Lord asked me, "Well then, how do you think I feel about you? If you as a father feel like that, then how much more do I feel and think about you?" He took me on a journey into his affections for me.

In another dream He asked me, "How does it feel when your children love you or care about your heart?" And I remembered how my children had tried to help me in my business when it was struggling, working all night with me, sleeping in the company van, because they just wanted to help me. I responded to the Lord that there was nothing better than when they cared for my heart.

He asked me another question, "How do you think I feel when you come after My heart?" He showed me how He felt when King David came after His heart, even in the midst of all his sin and weakness – His joy and pleasure was overwhelming.

Asking According to His Heart

As we say "yes" in our hearts to this "Call to the Wall," the first place God will take us is to the "Garden of Gethsemane," the place where He reveals His heart to us. Before we can truly co-labor with God "on the wall," we must "go the garden" to get His heart. He first wants to show us His heart for us. After that, He wants to show us what He cares about and His heart for others. We will never be truly effective in our prayer until we know His heart for us, for others and for Himself.

God spoke to me that our prayers are mostly very narcissistic – which means "in love with ourselves." Most of our prayers are selfish, focused on our personal needs, our desires, our cares, and our wants. And even when we pray for others, often we pray according to our limited understanding, our faulty opinions, and our flawed perspectives.

It is rare we ask Him what *His* desire is, and how *He* wants us to pray.

In one dream, I was bringing before God my long list of pressing, urgent needs. I was asking, proclaiming, praying scriptures, and beseeching God to take care of my litany of requests. Many of my requests were important and good. But it was "hamster-wheel" prayer – prayer without God's heart, without heavenly perspective and right understanding.

God suddenly turned to me and put up His hands motioning for me to stop, and with great intensity said, "SHHHHH! Stop! Stop everything! Enough of your narcissistic prayers! Enough praying out of your own understanding! Come listen to me, hear my heart, care about what I care about, and ask according to my will!"

We have such a "molehill view" of the world, versus God's "mountaintop view." As long as we see and ask from this small perspective, we can never ask rightly. The key to effective prayer is praying according to His heart and His will. When we ask according to selfish desires, we are not answered. As James 4:3 says, "You ask and you do not receive because you ask with wrong motives." In contrast, when we ask according to His heart and His desire, we know we will be answered – as 1 John 5:14-15 says, "If we ask anything according to His will He hears us…and we know we have the requests which we have asked from Him." This is the secret of powerful prayer. And not only do we have powerful prayer, but the true goal happens: we grow in intimacy with God, and the knowledge of His heart.

Going to the Garden

The Call to the Wall is a weighty invitation, it will mean giving our lives freely and fully to manning the wall – and yet the prize of gaining His heart far outweighs the cost.

I believe that if we choose to ignore this call, and just remain preoccupied with our own purposes, the Lord will give us over to our desires, and our hearts will harden, becoming dull to the knowledge of Him, and we will be offended in the shaking that is coming in the earth.

In the Garden of Gethsemane, Jesus invited His disciples to peer into His heart, saying "Come pray with me." When they did not, they fell into temptation, the very thing He had warned against.

Jesus told them, "pray that you might not enter into temptation." This was their invitation to the garden, and into His heart. They fell asleep, and in the hour of shaking that came, they were unable to stand. They fled Jesus at his crucifixion – perplexed and resentful. Their faith departed and they were unable to stand the storm than ensued.

If we choose our personal agendas over the Lord, we too will stumble in the day of shaking, just as the disciples did. We will stumble in at least three ways.

Three Stumblings

When the soldiers came for Jesus, Peter ran to fight and cut of the ear of one of the servants. Like Peter, if we do not "go to the garden" we will find ourselves fighting the wrong battles, completely unaware of what God is doing. In our ignorance, we end up actually opposing God! Peter was opposing Jesus going to the cross! Jesus rebuked him in John 18:11 saying, "Should I not drink this cup?"

The second stumbling of Peter was denying the Lord. In his "midnight hour" of testing, he lacked the faith and fortitude he needed to stand. If we don't "go to the garden," then like Peter, when we are at our point of crisis, we too will find only weakness in our souls. When our spiritual depths are truly plumbed, we will discover we are but a shallow well. Many of us, like Peter, think our zeal and commitment to God will sustain us – but zeal will always fail us. Only true intimacy with Jesus and personal love for Him, gained in the garden, will be sufficient to sustain us in our crisis hour.

The third stumbling of Peter was returning to fishing. The one who was to be a great apostle took on a completely wrong identity and purpose. In the day of his visitation, he was out of position. So too, if we do not go to the garden, in the day of our visitation, we will find ourselves out of divine position, walking in a wrong identity and purpose.

Three Graces

In one dream, God showed me three things that will happen, three graces we will receive when we "go to the garden" and obtain His heart. Jesus obtained these three graces. Had the disciples gone to the garden, they could have obtained them too.

The first grace we receive in the garden is the grace to forgive. Jesus had every right to be angry at those who crucified Him, but instead on the cross cried out, "Father, forgive them, for they know not what they do!" (Luke 23:34) Jesus was able to say this truly from His heart, even in the midst of the demonic storm raging around Him, because He had already won the battle in His heart, in the garden the night before.

The second grace we receive is the grace to surrender. Jesus was fully God, but He was also fully human. He knew He was going to die a horrible death, and He did not want to die. He prayed fervently in Luke 22:42 for the plan to be changed if it could be: "Father, if you are willing, remove this cup from me." Often the passage ordained for us by God is a bitter one, and we find ourselves unable and unwilling to embrace it. In the garden we obtain grace to surrender, where we can say in the deepest places in our heart as did Jesus, "not my will but yours be done" (Luke 22:42).

The third grace we receive is God's exhilarated, eternal view. Jesus' approaching crucifixion would be a time when darkness would reign, when Satan would rule, when evil would be fully manifest; when His chosen people would utterly reject Him; when His Father would call for His death; when His closest friends would desert Him; it would be a time of great personal pain and suffering. Yet, He in spite of this, He obtained a different view, a better view. He looked at these tragic events and found joy: "For the joy set before Him, He endured the cross." (Heb 12:2) Because of the garden, He was able to a see the glorious, exhilarated, eternal view of God and His grand purposes. This view is an altogether different view, by which we too can find joy, even in the darkest of times.

"Going to the garden" is essential before we get on the wall. We must know His heart, or we will be just a "noisy gong or a clanging cymbal." As we ask according to His heart and His will, we grow in the discovery of Him and our prayer life is completely transformed into a place of power from intimacy.

CHAPTER FOUR

the call to benevolence

As we go to the garden, God is going to begin to reveal His heart to us in many surprising and beautiful ways. The Lord showed me one area of His heart that He was going to open up to us in a significant way: benevolence.

The War We are In

Over a three month period in early 2000, I had a series of almost nightly dreams in which Jesus appeared as a man called "The Leader of Christianity." He was debriefing leaders on how the current world war was going – the "war" over the nature of God. He was speaking as the Central Commander specifically about different arenas of society where he wanted to bring a "healed" and "expanded" view of God – the eternal, priceless prize of the knowledge of the heart of God.

Jesus was not fully welcome in different arenas of life, yet God's heart was to bring change and begin to show his "forgotten faces" to and through them if they would heed his invitation and "ask again" for his heart. For example, He would show His face of "justice" in the political arena, and his face of "compassion" through the military arena. He wanted to show many more of His forgotten faces in the world of education, church, family, marketplace and youth.

Entrusted with the Weak and the Vulnerable

During these dreams I had one which seared my soul. It was a story my dad once told me of a show he'd seen on PBS. Now, years later I dreamed the story vividly.

A gentle–eyed Christian woman in her 80's was vividly recollecting the day, 40 years before, when she had been walking down the street of her hometown in Germany. The street was crowded with Jewish families being rounded up for a "census" by the Nazi soldiers. But in reality they were being counted and separated to be sent to their deaths in concentration camps. There was great wailing and anguish as families were being ripped apart.

A Jewish mother, holding the hand of her little girl as she waited in line, knowing she was about to lose her child, kept looking at the Christian woman every so often. She looked with such longing and kindness, as if she'd known her forever. The three of them were walking right next to each other, getting closer and closer to the front of the line, as the cries got louder and louder. Finally a soldier asked the Jewish mother harshly, "Is this your little girl?" She turned to the Christian woman with such large, trusting eyes, placed her little girl's hand into the woman's hand, and answered, "No, she's her little girl." Years later the Christian woman reflected, "I received that child as such a gift – I was entrusted with the most precious possession that mother had, and I raised her as my own."

In the dream, as I watched the lady get the hand of the little girl, suddenly the Jewish mother turned into Jesus, and the Christian lady turned into my older brother. The Lord said, "Because he has benevolence, stewardship and loves My heart, I can entrust the precious little girl to him." The picture kept changing from my brother into others who could also be entrusted. There were several past political leaders, including FDR, Truman, Kennedy, Churchill in the dream, and others too – but I was not one. The Lord said I couldn't be entrusted with the hand of the little girl. I would be unintentionally insensitive. The dream went through many people I knew, but there were just a few who could be trusted.

The Lord was revealing to me that the little girl, representing the weak and vulnerable ones, are His heart and His longing, and that in my current state I would be unintentionally insensitive, walking right past the deep level of her need, not seeing her pain. This was the treasure of his heart He wanted to give me.

The Lord Cares Deeply

I was reminded of a passage in Judges 9. The weak and vulnerable children of a nation have no one to care for them, and they go to the fruit trees to ask, "take care of us." The fruit trees refuse, saying, "we're too busy producing our own fruit." Then they go to the vines, who also refuse, saying "we're too busy drinking our own wine." Finally they ask the thorn bushes for help, who greedily agree, placing them into every form of slavery and abuse.

God showed me just a glimpse of his pain over the abuse of the vulnerable. He gave me a series of dreams about vulnerable ones that no one came to help. The next day after I had the dream about the little Jewish girl, I read a newspaper story about a local teenage boy who had killed his sister by beating her to death. That night I dreamed about it. I saw a little girl and an older boy brutally beating her, relentlessly pummeling her like a pro-wrestling dummy. I dreamed every feeling and question she had – her sense of worthlessness, loneliness and abandonment. I understood the Matthew 18:6 warning afresh – that it is better a millstone be tied around our necks than leave these vulnerable ones to their oppressor.

The Lord cares deeply about the weak and the vulnerable, those who cannot care for themselves. Every day He watches abuse and suffering, and it is not OK with Him. He wants us to care about what He cares about, and to share this burden with Him. God is benevolent, and He is calling us to be benevolent ones also. Webster's 1828 dictionary defines benevolence as, "The disposition to do good; good will; kindness; charitableness; the love of mankind, accompanied with a desire to promote their happiness." God is extending an invitation to us to realize our purpose in Him as His vehicle of benevolence, expressing His Father's heart of provision and protection for the vulnerable. God is looking for those who care about their suffering as He cares. He is looking for those who will "stand in the gap" before Him.

> [29]...they have wronged the poor and needy and have oppressed the sojourner without justice. [30]I searched for a man among them who would build up the wall and stand in the gap before Me... Ezekiel 22:29-30 (NASB)

This scripture paints a picture of a besieged city, whose wall has been breached and the enemy is pouring in through the breach. "Standing in the gap" refers to those who lay down their own lives and take position in the breach to personally fend off the enemy. This is those who spend their own precious time and resources to help those in need. God says this position is actually "before Him" – meaning that He too is in the gap and those who stand in the gap with Him will appear "before Him," having extraordinary access to Him.

Esther's Choice

In one dream, I dreamed of the present state of many in the marketplace. They were on the "Esther journey," meaning their lives are paralleling the life of Esther. This journey is not just for women, but men also. Today many of these are being presented with Esther's choice.

Esther started life as an orphan, in poverty and tragedy. But God in His kindness chose her and prepared her to serve in the court of the king. He blessed her greatly with wealth, honor and power. She acquired great skills and became an extraordinary leader, all because of the kindness of God.

Esther knew she was blessed and perhaps thought it was just for her. Then one day she realized that God had another reason too. There was a greater purpose for the favor and blessing that was on her life, that "for such as day as this" she was born. God asked her to use the blessing and favor He had given her to deliver others from suffering and death. God was offering her a choice: to lay her life down or watch her people be destroyed.

Many saints also started life in poverty and tragedy. But God in His kindness chose them and prepared them to serve in the courts of the king – the seats of earthly power and influence. He has blessed them greatly with wealth, honor and power. They have acquired great skills and have become extraordinary leaders, just because of the love and kindness of God.

Many have thought the blessing and favor on their lives was for them, because God loves them. But today God is knocking on their door and presenting them with Esther's choice: to lay their lives down and use their wealth and influence to help others. It is a high honor to be granted Esther's choice. It is an invitation to fellowship with Jesus and sharing in both His calling and His reward (Phil 3:10). It is an invitation to walk out the highest form of love possible, as did Jesus: "No greater love has anyone than this, that he lay his life down for his friends" (John 15:13). It is the opportunity to obtain the testimony of fulfilling the greatest commandments, to love God and love others (Matt 22:36-40).

This was a difficult choice for Esther. She did not feel particularly brave or suited for the task. She asked her people to pray and fast for her (Esther 4:14). Like those who prayed and fasted for Esther, we must pray and fast for believers in these places of wealth and influence in the marketplace, because the spiritual warfare over them will be intense.

We all remember our "first love" with God. But today many mature believers are being called into "second love." First love is sweet, but second love is deep. Those on the Esther journey are today being called into a second love – a love that is deep and costly.

Esther's choice, to lay down her life, made her realize that her love relationship with the king was not where it needed to be. She must deepen her love with the king. She held two "banquets of wine," for the purpose of renewing her love. So too God is coming to many today and asking them, "Do you love me?" Many saints today have become like the Ephesus church: they are full of good deeds, but without a living, vibrant, love relationship. Jesus said, "This I have against you, that you have left your first love" (Rev 2:4). God has not the slightest interest in good works apart from a love relationship

(Rev 2:5). He is calling us, like He did Esther and Ephesus, to renew love.

Our Current Condition

Today's saints are in danger of being unintentionally insensitive, retreating after our first try at benevolence, leaving the vulnerable to suffering and exploitation.

The Leader of Christianity showed me in the debriefings that he'd given many groups of Christians marching orders of benevolence, and they had moved out, beginning to do large acts of benevolence. He told me about groups from California, Canada, Texas and Florida. However, they had met fierce resistance from the enemy which they had not been trained to overcome.

They met cheating, theft and loss, from inside and outside. The enemy wanted to trap them in pain, perplexity and offense, as described in Chapters 1 and 2. They retreated into insecurity and self-protection, weakness and sin, content to concentrate on their own gain. In the words of the Leader of Christianity, they had gotten "tilted." He said that being "tilted" was OK, so long as they didn't stay there and justify themselves, pretending they weren't tilted.

Second Commissioning Starts with "Asking Again".

The first moves into benevolence had been motivated by excitement to "do something big for God," in duty and zeal. In His mercy, the Lord wanted to lead us through this into a deeper, truer, and more costly love, like He did with Peter when He restored him in John 21:15-19. I believe the Lord is now issuing an invitation to a second commissioning.

This second commissioning can only begin with dusting ourselves off and "asking again" for his heart, as described in Chapter 1. If we do this, the fear of God will come, and in his kindness He will lead us to repentance for our insensitivity and retreating into a mission of personal gain, and he would wash us and cleanse us.

Recognition and repentance are the path to this second commissioning and the privilege of "taking the hand of the little girl," sharing in and expressing the compassionate heart of God for the weak and the vulnerable.

In the next chapter, we will look at another area of God's heart He wants to reveal in this hour: His desire for intimacy with His people.

CHAPTER FIVE

intimacy with God

Our Only Refuge is Intimacy with God

Shortly after Terry and I were married, we moved to Zimbabwe as
missionaries on a farm. I was somewhat a spiritual "hotshot." I felt
strong, zealous, confident and deeply principled as a minister. But
when I arrived I discovered that lawlessness reigned in the nation
and that dissidents were threatening the lives of all of us, who were
missionaries. Faced with a very real life and death crisis, my faith
waned; I was gripped by fear and insecurity. I didn't know if God
would deliver us. I didn't know what he thought about me or my
situation. I suddenly knew I didn't know Him very well at all. I
began seeking God to know Him like I never had before.

Many believers today think they have a strong faith. But in the
shakings that are coming, they too will find their faith empty of
substance. This is because our faith is based in head knowledge and
propped up by our support systems. True faith is based in a deep
personal intimacy with God, a cultivated knowledge of God, and life
history of trust. For example, this is what Daniel, Shadrach,

Meshach, and Adebnego had – they were unshaken when facing a horrible death before an enraged king.

This is the hour for believers to develop a deep personal intimacy with God, and to cultivate a true knowledge of God in our hearts. This is the only way we will be able to stand in the days ahead. And not only will we stand, but we will prosper and thrive.

In 1989 my wife and I were in South Africa, which was in the grip of apartheid and much violence. I dreamt one night of a city in panic and chaos – it resembled what we've seen recently in hurricane-ravaged New Orleans. In the dream I was overcome by a sense of panic. I was solely concerned with my own family's needs for food, water and safety. I discovered that all my cultivated history in God was insufficient at that hour. In fact, I completely lost the reality of my Christian foundation. I found that I had Christian practices and principles aplenty, but without the substance of a near relationship with God, I had nothing.

Then in the dream, in the chaotic darkness of the city, someone walked up to me, placed their hand in mine and said, "It's not *what* you know in the days to come, but *who* you know" (John 1:38-42). I knew it was the Son of God and that I needed to know Him, rather than just know more about Him. My personal relationship with Him needed to become truly substantial. Many know much about the Lord, but it is quite different to know him closely and intimately.

I was profoundly humbled in that moment. It broke my heart to realize that at the point of crisis I did not have the ability to believe He was my source. I had looked to myself. A huge transformation began to occur in me. Over the next 4-5 months, my distant, unclear knowledge about God became real. I moved from "knowing Him from afar" to "knowing Him so near" and all my learning about Him became intimate, personal and very specific in nature (Job 42:5). I wasn't wondering or unsure about Him anymore. I became confident in Jesus, that He was all I needed. My panic turned into peace. (Isa. 26:3)

Four Forgotten Faces of God

I became aware of Him in four very specific ways. First I saw Him as "The God who Sees and Cares". I saw how He cared for me. I looked back through my history now with His eyes and His view. I saw His concern and care for me throughout my entire life and His tenderness towards me. I now knew the God that had never left or forsaken me.

I also saw Him as the "God of Eternal Joy," that He has an exhilarated, eternal view that everything was going to turn out right and best. I saw that His nature was resounding joy, and that His plan brought ultimate joy. He was unchanging and He could be my joy in all things.

Third, He revealed Himself as the "Fiercely Dedicated God," that not only had he seen and cared like a friend but He was like a protective big brother, that in times of adversity He would fight for me against my enemies, even if it would cost Him His life (Proverbs 18:24).

Finally, I saw that He was the "God of All of Life." I used to think I had to escape to the temple to be safe and find God, but now I knew He was the God who would be with me in all my everyday life; He was truly the God who is "all in all" (1 Corinthians 15:28) across the city and who expertly knows how to navigate the city. I saw Him coming powerfully as the glorious King in Psalm 24, coming to take His rightful place on the throne, into the gates of the city and into every arena of life:

⁷ Lift up your heads, O gates,
And be lifted up, O ancient doors,
That the King of glory may come in!
⁸ Who is the King of glory?
The LORD strong and mighty,
The LORD mighty in battle.
⁹ Lift up your heads, O gates,
And lift them up, O ancient doors,
That the King of glory may come in!
¹⁰ Who is this King of glory?
The LORD of hosts,
He is the King of glory.
Psalms 24:7-10 (NASB)

Feeding Others on the Knowledge of God

A profound transformation had happened for me in that dream and now I was ready to help others. In the dream I was led to other parts of the city where there were multitudes of people in panic and I was able to proclaim this new-found intimate knowledge of who God is. I started to proclaim these forgotten faces of God from a place of personal reality rather than theory. I then would put their hands into His hand and soon they began to see for themselves. These people started to move from terror to perfect peace and intimate knowledge.

I wasn't a trained preacher, a professional minister or seminary student. I was just an "ordinary one." But I realized that I had gained a unique personal experience about who God was, and therefore I had become a voice for Him. He showed me that my voice, and the voice of each and every one of us who cultivate the knowledge of God, was immeasurably valuable in the effect it had on people. I and others had become proclaimers of His heart and of the true knowledge of God.

Watchmen Who Guard the Promises

In the dream I saw there were many who were proclaiming good Christian practices and principles, but at that time I couldn't see any who were proclaiming the intimate knowledge of the heart of God in the present-tense circumstances.

Then in later dreams the Lord showed me some others on the street corners who were proclaiming the knowledge of God with their own unique voice, and how valuable that voice was to Him and to others. To the youth He had shown himself as the God who sees and cares, to the elderly as the fiercely dedicated God, to the housewife as the God of eternal joy and to the marketplace people as the God of all of life.

These proclaimers are really the watchmen over the cities – they have the privileged position of guarding the cities by proclaiming the intimate faces of God that have been specifically revealed to them – the truth of who God is and His promises.

Proclaimers of His Heart

In another dream He showed me a city, and in the midst of all the activity, how He was not perceived there (the city represented the every day life in all of its diversity and complexity). Many people were dying in their own efforts because they didn't have the right focus on him or an intimate knowledge of his heart. They had ministries, callings, causes, strategies, principles, and practices, but they hadn't considered him.

They had made the Kingdom of God about works and callings instead of about Him. I saw how God was lovesick for friendship with His people, that they might perceive him, and they might know

His heart. He was deeply pained that people were dying without a true image of Him, never knowing His burning heart of love for them. Instead He was perceived as cold, distant, angry, or hard, the God with the "white glove," the God with impossible expectations.

I recently heard a heart–breaking story of a believing, bright young medical student, who after a long evening of study, crawled to the open window at the end of her bed and purposefully slipped out of the window, falling to her death four floors below.

A few nights later I dreamed her thoughts – the pressure she was under, how her parents had always been disappointed with her, and her wrong view of God as one who was always disappointed in her. As she was falling, there was a moment of recognition of what she had done. Then in the dream a pair of hands came out of the window and caught her ankles, bringing her back up and saving her life.

People are wasting their lives on foolish pursuits, and in some cases even dying because they have a wrong view of God. This Call to the Wall is to gain his heart, to care about what he cares for, and to call out to see the true knowledge of God restored to all the arenas of life: that people would no longer flee from him, pursuing their own damaging agendas; and that people would no longer believe the lies about God, and like the student, lose hope. Through our prayer on the wall, we can grab them by their ankles, partnering with God in His desires for them.

Partners in Prayer

I believe there is currently a holy invitation for us to peer into the heart of God as we respond to the Call to the Wall. This call is to stand with a new, true view of him and his promises, to fight in prayer for those who cannot fight for themselves, and to pray for the messages and messengers of the heart of God to go forth.

As we obtain the true knowledge of God for our own lives and then become proclaimers of this knowledge to others, we will shine like stars, as Daniel 12:3 says: "Those who have insight will shine brightly like the brightness of the expanse of heaven, and those who lead the many to righteousness, like the stars forever and ever."

As we have seen, God is taking His people through a process: asking again, becoming sons of Jacob, getting His heart, and reclaiming intimacy. He is preparing us for His next big step – redeeming our cities.

CHAPTER SIX

a vision of redeemed cities

In 1983 I had an open vision that profoundly impacted my life and set the direction of my life ever since. The vision was very long and had several parts – the last part was a vision of a redeemed city.

Jesus Unperceived in the City

At first I saw an ordinary city as it was today. The city was full of activity. In homes and businesses, jobs and workplaces, educational institutions and government offices, His people were busy about their daily affairs. They were working and playing, laughing and crying, worrying and striving – but there was a profound sense of emptiness about it all. In the midst of the city Jesus was walking as the "light of the world" (John 1:5), doing marvelous works here and there, but no one noticed Him – He was completely unperceived.

Though He was doing works, they were unaware. His heart was reaching out to the city longing to gather them to Himself. It was like

Matt 23:37: "Jerusalem, Jerusalem…How often I wanted to gather your children together, the way a hen gathers her chicks under her wings." He missed them and they missed Him but they were unaware of Him and couldn't see Him. Some looked for Him from time to time, but couldn't see Him.

Jesus walked alone in the midst of the city. Even though He was there in the midst of their daily affairs, He was excluded from them, because they didn't perceive Him and they didn't invite Him in. He was lonely and lovesick for the companionship of His beloved people.

Jesus had many people in the city that were filled with purpose but not desirous of His presence. They were good and moral but not after the Man Christ Jesus. They were diligent, but out of duty rather than desire for Him. Jesus was crying out to them, "I see your works but your hearts are far from me and you don't know how to bring them close."

They were poor worshippers. Though they turned their hearts to Him once a week on Sunday, all their daily affairs, the majority of their lives, they never gave to Him, or turned toward Him in the midst of it. Jesus longed for true worshippers that He could love and who would love Him back. He longed for those who would begin to look for Him in the midst of the city, like His beloved bride in Song of Songs 3:2: "I must arise now and go about the city; in the streets and in the squares I must seek him whom my soul loves." He just wanted simple devotion (2 Cor. 11:3) and friendship with His people in the midst of the city. He knew it was such an easy yoke for them, and that in doing it, everything else in their lives would become meaningful and joyful.

Jesus also longed to be a friend to sinners (Matt 11:19). He wanted to be with the tax-collectors, the politicians, the educators, the government workers, and the business people because they were to be His family too.

Forerunners Arise

Then I saw people in the city who started to "get it" – they started to perceive Him and started to believe they could walk with Him in all of their life. They began to get excited and started to think about building a glorious new city with His name over it. But when they did, suddenly tsunamis began crashing over them and they started to drown. The tsunamis represented difficult circumstances, the worries and cares of life, and the clutter in their lives. Many of them had never really believed for a relationship with Him in all of life. Others were still living in shame, believing their issues and circumstances were bigger than Jesus. Many felt like they could live out some of His principles but they were not worthy to live in His presence – like the prodigal son in Luke 15:11-31, as described in Chapter 2.

But then I saw the most glorious thing happen: they saw Jesus and they saw His eyes of love and desire for them, His fierce dedication to them, and His good plan for them. Once they saw His eyes, they could no longer live without Him. They had tasted of Him and saw that He was good (Ps. 34:8) in the city and in all of their lives and they were ruined for anything less.

They began to lift up a cry like Patrick Henry who declared, "Give me liberty or give me death!" Only their cry was, "Give me intimacy and relationship with You in all of life, or give me death!" Desire for Him had been awakened – a desire that could not be denied and that pushed everything else to second place.

They began to get the "advanced tools" they needed to swim through the tsunamis to the shore. Some of the advanced tools were the things we have written about in earlier chapters: asking again in faith, becoming sons of Jacob, going to the Garden to get His heart, intimacy with Jesus, and getting on the wall with others.

They began to shout out Psalm 24, for the King of Glory to make His triumphal entry into the city and into all of their lives. They were no longer satisfied with living by good principles. They were no longer satisfied with having a good purpose or calling – all of life, every breath, had to be about Him.

They became like Paul in Philippians 3:8, saying, "I count all my accomplishments, and my entire ministry as dung compared to the surpassing value of knowing You!" They let go of their bitterness and depression, their doubts about themselves. They let go of their own personal agendas, because they were no longer important.

Some responded like Moses in Ex 33:15, saying, "I can't go unless you come with me!" Some responded like David in Ps 44, saying, "It's only the light of Your Presence that saves me. I wilt, I deteriorate without seeing You!" Some responded like Jeremiah in Jeremiah 9:23-24, saying, "I cannot boast except in God alone, who exercises lovingkindness, justice, and righteousness in the earth!" Some responded like Cyrus in Isaiah 44:28, saying, "Let a glorious city be built, a dwelling place for Your Presence and Your Name!" Some responded like Nehemiah in Nehemiah 1-2, saying, "You must have a city with Your Name!"

These forerunners became uniquely committed to searching out and proclaiming His promises over their cities. They became studiers of Him and His affection, His joy, His benevolence, His creativity, His plans for the city and the marketplace. They couldn't bear to not know Him fully. They refused to allow Him to not be loved. They refused to allow Him to be ignored. They were so lovesick for Him and appreciative of Him. They longed for Him and His promises, longed to understand His heart and experience Him completely.

They were the pioneers of practical intimacy – everyday intimacy in everyday life. They were determined to find Him, and they would succeed. They would experience the "pioneer fade" at times, getting weary because of the opposition. But they had crossed over, where they were totally and completely given over to be special friends of Him in all of life.

Love for Jesus

It started with the forerunners, but soon He began to be perceived by the many. Then it was like the Father pulled back the veil on His Son, and they saw Him all over the city and the people had no other thought but to praise Him.

He revealed Himself as in Isaiah 6:1, with a beauty high and lifted up; and as in Revelation 1:12-18, His majesty all-consuming of John's heart; and as in Revelation 5:13, where His loveliness, His unveiled majesty and glory subdued hearts. He was altogether lovely (Song 5:16). His loveliness had overwhelming drawing power. The power of His revealed presence and the intimate knowledge of Him produced a consuming, passionate love from all, and humility reigned.

This is when Psalm 67 happened. When they saw Him, and His ways, then all the people praised Him. What a city this became as they became captivated by Him.

Benevolent Ones Emerge

I saw Jesus in the city and He was overflowing, abundant in generosity and benevolence. His heart so loved people, He so valued them, He saw them with such great worth, they were so precious to Him. I was astounded by the way He looked at people. I was undone by who he was in care and affection and benevolence towards human beings.

The leaders of the city and the business people began to realize how they had missed His heart. He longed to give everything to His children. He was the God who was the cheerful giver (2 Cor 7:38). He was the giver of every good gift (James 1:17). But they had misrepresented His very heart. His nature was being denied. Their giving had become obligatory, compulsory, detached from their hearts. They had become resentful and skeptical in their giving. They would sit in their ivory towers and occasionally drop a check for a need but it was a violation of God's nature.

In this city, as they began to see His heart for the vulnerable and the needy; they got captured by His heart, His love, His benevolence, His very nature. Their hearts became infected by His love. They began to wake up and come alive to His heart of benevolence versus their pitiful self concern.

They were transformed like Ebenezer Scrooge in "A Christmas Carol." They went from the first Scrooge, dehumanizing work and money, and doing business based on fear and greed, to the second Scrooge after he got the picture of true love and the difference he could make. They got the "Tiny Tim" revelation, where their hearts got focused on God's heart and the good they could do for the orphan, widow and the "least among them."

They started to view money differently, not for what it could do for them, but what it could do for others. They started to view success differently. It wasn't about getting their "gold," money and success, but it was about a deeper invitation into the treasure of God's benevolent heart. They started to live out Job 22:24-25:

> [24] [If you] place your gold in the dust,
> And the gold of Ophir among the stones of the brooks,
> [25] Then the Almighty will be your gold
> And choice silver to you.
> Job 22:24-25 (NASB)

They placed their earthly Gold "in the dust" and the Almighty became their gold. And like Scrooge, they found themselves when they found His heart of benevolence.

Cities Transformed

The city was also being transformed in other ways. People began to live out the Sermon on the Mount lifestyle in everyday life. Many willingly and joyfully began to give all that they had for one another. People became a loving community like the first century church.

People so enjoyed each other in the city and the marketplace. They celebrated the uniqueness of each other. There was great unity even in the midst of great diversity. Understanding came first before judgment. People loved each other's different expressions of life.

There was another name over the city which was the "Lift You Up" city, where true brotherhood ruled. The norm became caring for one another and fighting for one another's hearts and destinies.

This city was unsurpassed in affection. People really preferred others as more important than themselves. They saw each other through the eyes of Jesus, which made love easy. They were like Paul who said, "You are like my very own heart" (Philemon 1:12).

The love of God and the love for people was so strong, it led to extravagant giving. The outflow was amazing miracles of love.

I saw this lead to the restoration of joy and celebration because this love cast out fear and caused the petty and critical spirit to flee. Magnanimous spirits ruled because love was bigger than the little things. People belly-laughed for days on end because they knew evil was here for only a moment and joy would last forever in the city.

There was a discovery of happy purpose. Those who had been melancholy didn't fear the future any more, but smiled at it because they knew in Him they would always win. All of life became an adventure into intimacy with Jesus, whether in struggles and challenges or not.

This city had a feeling of oasis. It had such an amazing quality: divine rest. So many had been driven by their demons and struggles, and could not find a moment's rest – but now they could recline with Jesus and be replenished. Life was refreshing.

Families became centers of God's fame. Each had a unique banner over it, its own special-ness which was regained in this city.

There was hearing of God's heart in the city. People refused to "build their own fires" of empty human initiative, but honored His heart and His desires. There would be such sensitivity to what He desired.

These were new expressions of Christianity in the marketplace. The people said, "No more to the fear and greed model. No more to big egos. No more ignoring God's desires. 'Yes' to being leaders in asking God and being dependent upon God. 'Yes' to being leaders in generosity. 'Yes' to being leaders in love and loving God through our work."

CHAPTER SEVEN

call to the wall

So far, we have looked at some of the areas of our lives God is forging in this hour: asking and trusting; wrestling over the promises; glimpsing His heart; and intimacy with Him. We have also explored some of the purposes of His heart being established at this time: extravagant benevolence and redeemed cities.

These are all to prepare to stand with hearts that thrive in the midst of the turmoil and testing. I believe in this hour, the storm clouds of culture and chaos are gathering. Rage, entitlement, cold-heartedness, greed, arrogance, intolerance, and lack of love rule the day and are gaining strength. The Lord is strongly calling his people to the "wall" of intercession, both individually and corporately, to find his heart – for ourselves as individuals, for our cities, and for those dying without the true knowledge of him.

The Prophet Joel wrote some years before the Babylonians invaded Judah. Joel called the people to wholeheartedness, prayer and fasting, and the true knowledge of God:

> [12] "Return to Me with all your heart,

And with fasting, weeping and mourning;
¹³ And rend your heart and not your garments."
Now return to the LORD your God,
For He is gracious and compassionate,
Slow to anger, abounding in lovingkindness
Joel 2:12-13 (NASB)

We are to come to God *because He is gracious and compassionate, slow to anger and abounding in lovingkindness.* All the earlier chapters of this book can be summed up in these two verses above. God is truly passionate for us, and we are to lay hold of Him and His heart, and return to Him with our whole heart.

Joel then called the nation "to the wall" of wholehearted prayer and intercession:

¹⁵ Blow a trumpet in Zion,
Consecrate a fast, proclaim a solemn assembly,
¹⁶ Gather the people, sanctify the congregation,
Assemble the elders,
Gather the children and the nursing infants.
Let the bridegroom come out of his room
And the bride out of her bridal chamber.
¹⁷ Let the priests, the LORD'S ministers,
Weep between the porch and the altar,
And let them say, "Spare Your people, O LORD,
And do not make Your inheritance a reproach,
A byword among the nations.
Why should they among the peoples say,
'Where is their God?'"
Joel 2:15-17 (NASB)

I believe we are entering into a Joel 2 time. God is calling for his people to gather together to call out for His divine purposes and mandates to be established in the earth.

Floods Coming

Since 2002 I've had dreams of floods coming to America, people drowning and in dire need of "advanced spiritual tools" to get to the shore where the promises lay. The primary advanced spiritual tool was prayer according to his heart – to "shush," stopping everything, stopping our narcissistic prayers, and start caring about what he cares about in prayer. During the storms, we were to "look up" (Luke 21:28), remembering and reclaiming his promises, and we would have the strength to swim to shore.

Rage or Repent

In August of 2005 I had a dream where thousands of people were standing on the edge of a cliff, only to be blown off and fall thousands of feet. On the way down they were losing all the earthly things that were of value to them – houses, material possessions, pet sins, etc. – things that had become idols to them, imprisoning their hearts. As they hit the ground, to my surprise they survived! They landed, with great loss, but also freed of things that had become a prison to them. They stood up, and divested of every distraction, they faced God.

At this point they either raged against God in offense at what he had taken, or tenderly, joyfully repented and turned back towards him, saying he was enough. Some were freed of life-long sins and bondages, getting wonderfully set free into the liberty of Christ. Some became radically abandoned to God.

Cities Having New Starts

Where people and cities chose repentance and turned back to God, Christianity that looked like the Book of Acts broke out. It was like the "Jesus Movement" of the 1970's in terms of radical abandonment, love, and the manifest presence of God. It had the added ingredient of wisdom – it was mature, focused, and strategic.

This led to cities having fresh starts in God and his ways – it looked phenomenal. There would be immediate results and we would be amazed at the righteousness that would be birthed, even in unlikely places like the political arena. In fact, it started in the political arena, moving into the marketplace, and then to the church.

People would have businesses that became "houses of light" where miracles of compassion and benevolence would happen. Flowing from God's love, salvations, deliverance and healings would occur there in the midst of day-to-day business. Lawyers and judges were adjudicating justice with a righteous spirit like Phineas, doing what was right for the people, not acting out of greed or rage at the system. Doctors received a completely different vision for their practices – not just healing centers, but centers of the "habitation of God." Sales people became "sent agents of God" with his heart; they were being led by the spirit, going into buildings, delivering people and leading them to salvation.

And so touching to God's heart, the weak and vulnerable were being cared for (as described in Chapter 4) and God was being loved in the cities.

Storms Coming

I have had several dreams in 2005 of tsunamis and storms coming to several different cities. We will see natural cataclysmic events that will in effect push many off the cliff as I saw in the dream, into rage or repentance.

I believe hurricane Katrina in New Orleans was one such event, and God was inviting the city to a new start. In my dream I saw many in the inner city who were held captive in poverty and a systemic corruption of soul. The young were being schooled in sin and led into a lifestyle of the deepest corruption even before their consciences could develop. God showed me that he was going to lift the skirt on evil and expose it. The storm has flushed people out of these situations, many being re-housed in righteous homes, to give them a new start.

Many see what has happened as an obstacle rather than an opportunity, but could this be the redemptive goodness and grace of God? In the dream the different idolatries that kept people bound and devoid of true life – be it money, music, whiskey, sports teams, pornography, etc., were being freed from them by the force of the floods and the storms, and they were beginning to feel their heart come alive in God again – it was an amazing transformation.

I saw around 12,000 people come out of this with a new view of God, empowered to help change New Orleans. I believe it is possible that in the future other whole cities could turn to the Lord in a single day.

Tinkers

I saw some people would be commissioned and released at this time to become "tinkers of God" to these devastated areas. Tinkers were medieval craftsmen and merchants who traveled into remote areas bringing needed goods. These "tinkers of God" were in some cases businesspeople who would bring their business crafts and services into these areas, but also take their spiritual wares like divine perspective, wisdom, faith and divine strategies to rebuild. They would take these things to those that didn't have them and share them door to door. Some of them were the "proclaimers of His heart" I wrote about in Chapter 5.

He Wants to be Discovered in Cities

For over 20 years now the Lord has given me dreams of cities being redeemed and restored to the true knowledge of Him (John 4:23-24). As I described in the previous chapter, these cities would become centers of God's habitation (Psalm 107) and His presence, and His ways would be known in all the arenas of life throughout the city, not just in the church (Jeremiah 33:10-11, Ps 24). What I saw was so incredible in these cities that my faith sometimes had a hard time reaching for it. Then I felt the Lord whispering to me, "Tell the Hebrides Islands this doesn't work! Tell Wales this doesn't work! Tell New York, Guatemala and Azusa Street this doesn't work!" I believe if we will get "on the wall" of prayer and ask again for the new view of God's plan and purposes, we will see the God who is able and who desires to bring forth these redeemed cities.

Calling the City Watchmen

I had a powerful encounter where I was instructed in a dream that we were to get a thousand saints together to cry out for the people falling from the cliff – whether in New Orleans or elsewhere. We were to cry out for angelic escorts to escort them into grace to make the right decision. It is now the time to co–labor with God's heart and be His instruments to release grace upon the planet, according to Ps 115:16: "The heaven, even the heavens, are the Lord's; but the earth He has given to the children of men."

I saw thousands of footprints with people's names on them. These were those who were to come together and station themselves to be a people after God's own heart and to be voices crying in the wilderness for God's promises in the marketplace and in the city. It was a time like in Judges 5, where all the tribes were to come together for the cause of the Lord – a cause bigger than their differences or their own personal purposes.

Prayer, I believe is what will make the difference between whether people will rage or repent. We are in a serious hour, and we have a privileged invitation to pray, to get on the wall again like the watchmen and pray people through to repentance, and into a new view of God.

Many we would pray for would not know how to repent – their spiritual dullness was so deep. The Lord has such compassion not to leave them there. If we would pray on their behalf, God would release grace for people to choose him and repent. I saw that angelic escorts were the only hope – and that if we got on the wall, God would release angelic escorts and whole cities would repent and get fresh starts, but if we didn't, they would rage, and be worse than before.

What the Watchmen will Cry Out

In this hour, I believe we are all called to be such watchmen who cry out, and the Lord has highlighted Isaiah 62:1-7 to me as the process of equipping us:

Isaiah 62:1a, "For Zion's sake I will not keep silent," – for Zion's sake, for the Church's sake we are not to keep silent. We are to cry out first for the Church. We are to ask again for his kingdom to come here.

Isaiah 62:1b, "For Jerusalem's sake I will not remain quiet." For Jerusalem's sake – which is the city – we are not to keep silent. We are to cry out also for His kingdom to come in the city - our own city and all the arenas of everyday life.

Isaiah 62:1c, "Until her righteousness shines out like the dawn, her salvation like a blazing torch." For our righteousness to shine, we must have a right view of our own history in God. We need to reinterpret our circumstances according to His goodness instead of according to our pain and rejection. When we look back through the "book of remembrance" of our lives, revisiting our history according to His goodness, establishing a foundation of thankfulness in our hearts, then the light of our salvation begins to burn.

Isaiah 62:2 "The nations will see your righteousness, and all kings your glory; you will be called by a new name that the mouth of the Lord will bestow." I believe that new name is "HOPE" – House of Prayer for Everyone, where everyone's unique cry is vital.

Isaiah 62:3 "You will be a crown of splendor in the Lord's hand, a royal diadem in the hand of your God." We will become His authoritative instrument, the royal diadem. We begin to see our worth, how beautiful our cries are to him, and the power of our cries before the throne.

Isaiah 62:4 "No longer will they call you Deserted or your name Desolate. But you will be called Hephzibah (my delight is in her) and your land Beulah (married); for the Lord will take delight in you, and your land will be married." Here now the Lord promises to prosper our "land," our portion in life (our sphere of influence). We are to believe again for our cities, the land where we walk, our jobs, businesses and workplaces, and this cry will bring forth the promises.

Isaiah 62:5 "As a young man marries a maiden, so will your sons marry you; as a bridegroom rejoices over his bride, so will your God rejoice over you." We will know His pleasure and joy over us in the process, like newlyweds – our prayers will be the sweet, intimate asking of a bride rather than the distant plaintive begging of the widow of Luke 18:3.

Isaiah 62:6 "I have posted watchmen on your walls, O Jerusalem; they will never be silent day or night. You who call on the LORD, give yourselves no rest," This empowered cry, rooted in the remembrance of fulfilled promises and seeing our history through His eyes, is a place of asking that greatly delights the Lord. So often He has wanted to act, but was uninvited and unable to act because we didn't ask Him or we gave up asking after a time. He is so delighted to have a company of confident askers, who ask according to His heart and release Him to act in the earth.

A Solemn Call

This Call to the Wall as watchmen, being proclaimers of His true nature, is a privileged and serious one. I believe there is now an invitation going forth to these watchmen to watch and pray with Him in the "Garden of Gethsemane." This call to the garden is an attitude of watching with Jesus and learning what His heart cares about. It is to prepare us for our calling as watchmen over the cities.

CHAPTER EIGHT

getting on the wall

I believe God is calling His people to "the wall" of intercession, via "the garden" of intimacy and the knowledge of His heart. God is calling everyone: businesspeople, students, workers, stay-at-home moms & dads and retirees; He is calling pastors, prophets, and ministers.

The Lord is issuing a powerful decree to get on the wall in this hour. In one stunning dream I saw the Lord issuing this decree to rally His people for battle in the same manner Saul did 3000 years ago:

> [6]Then the Spirit of God came upon Saul mightily when he heard these words, and he became very angry. [7]He took a yoke of oxen and cut them in pieces, and sent them throughout the territory of Israel by the hand of messengers, saying, "Whoever does not come out after Saul and after Samuel, so shall it be done to his oxen." Then the dread of the LORD fell on the people, and they came out as one man. 1 Samuel 11:6-7 (NASB)

God is drafting people who will take the Isa 62:7 pledge, to be those "who will give Him no rest until He establishes and makes Jerusalem a praise in the earth."

What is the Call-to-the-Wall?

I believe one of the first steps we must take is to be a part of national Call to the Wall gatherings. These gatherings are for us to get "on the wall" and cry out together and to lay out practical "onramps" for people to pray. The goal is that steadfast, anointed prayer becomes attainable for everyone. The International House of Prayer (www.ihop.org) in Kansas City will be regularly hosting such events.

Secondly, we must begin regular prayer, both corporately and individually. Many people are committing to pray 5 days per week, 2 hours per day. Those who are unable to do the full two hours are committing one hour per day. And those unable to do that are committing to pray at least weekly. People can either start their own prayer gathering, or find one online (www.calltothewall.com) and join it. Those who are unable do either of these can join live prayer online.

Finally, we are asking people to fast one day per week. Many people are fasting together every Tuesday. Those unable to do a water fast can fast solid food, or anything that works for their lives.

Houses of Prayer

In the early 1980's God began to speak to many church leaders about prayer. Paul Yonggi Cho in Korea, Mike Bickle in Kansas City, and hundreds of others across the nations responded and began to embrace prayer in a committed way.

In Kansas City, God spoke supernaturally to Mike Bickle and the leadership of the Kansas City Fellowship about prayer. He said that there would be 24/7 prayer and worship in the "spirit of the tabernacle of David." In 1999, Mike was led to start the International House of Prayer, a 24/7 worship and prayer center. Today there are several hundred full-time staff "prayer missionaries" whose main job is prayer. The 84 prayer meetings per week are open to everyone.

Today there are dozens of similar houses of prayer, many going 24/7. These houses of prayer are being used strategically by the Lord to restore the grace of intense, steadfast prayer and fasting. They play an important role in envisioning, training, and producing tools and helps to empower the burgeoning global prayer movement.

HOPE Churches

I saw thousands of churches renaming themselves as HOPE churches: "Houses of Prayer for Everyone."

In a powerful dream in 2003, Jesus as "the leader of Christianity" was addressing church pastors. He looked at them and said, "My church has become centers of teaching, entertainment, and mobilizing." My first thought was that these were good things, but then he shook His head sadly and continued, "But this should not be. My church is to be a place of encounter with God. A cold heart should not be able to enter my church cold and leave cold." He was not talking about fiery preaching, but individual hearts being touched by the presence of God and prayer.

I believe God is getting ready to change the status quo in churches. In a recent dream, God spoke to me about pastors, telling me that over the next few years our pastors would be the heroes, leading the people of God into wholehearted, steadfast prayer. I believe churches will turn into "marveling centers," marveling at the Son of God, and they will be transformed into places of encounter with God – but it may be that the encounter will happen in the prayer times more than the Sunday services. Several churches I know have started doing this, and after several years, have begun to experience extraordinary growth, spiritual vitality, and young adults streaming in and becoming wholehearted.

HOPE churches are those that place strong emphasis on regular, sustained prayer and fasting, and that host prayer meetings for everyone at least 5 days per week. I believe thousands of churches will begin to do this, and in so doing they will become places of encounter with God rather than just teaching, entertainment and mobilizing centers.

Biz-HOPs

As earlier spoken of, I saw the "Jesus movement" of the 1970's returning, and in particular coming to businesses. I saw prayer, evangelism, and miracles coming to boardrooms, and an army of sold-out businesspeople living lives of spiritual abandonment.

Businesspeople all over the world are being drawn to prayer. In daily office prayer meetings, believers are gathering and praying for the Kingdom of God to come in their workplaces and cities. 2 Chronicles 7:14 is a well-known verse, but with hidden meaning:

> [14]If My people who are called by My name humble themselves and pray and seek My face and turn from their wicked ways, then I will hear from heaven, will forgive their sin and will heal their land. 2 Chronicles 7:14 (NASB)

In the Bible, "land" was business, because it referred to farming and grazing. So this verse specifically applies to business. If the believers in a business gather together and pray for it, they have great spiritual authority there. We do not need to try to gather or influence unbelievers, but just the believers – "If *My people*, who are called by *My name*..." God will grant great authority to His people to establish His Kingdom through prayer, even if they are a small minority.

I encourage believers in the workplace to find the other believers and start a prayer meeting. Even the most secular businesses will often allow use of a meeting room before work or at lunch time, and will send a notice of the meeting to employees. "Politically-correct" organizations feel compelled to offer a Christian group space if they offer space to any other group. The prayer meeting should be primarily for prayer. I know this sounds redundant, but I have been to a lot of "prayer breakfasts" where there is a lot more breakfast than prayer! I encourage them to ask specifically for the Kingdom of God to come in their midst. If they can gather substantially all the believers, then God will come and "heal" the business. One of the advantages of being in the marketplace is that believers from completely opposite church backgrounds and traditions usually have little trouble coming into unity for prayer. Many believers have tried to start Bible studies at work, which can be positive, but prayer is the only way to bind the believers together in unity, to meet the requirements of 2 Chron. 7:14, and to fulfill what Jesus told us to do to establish His Kingdom: "*Pray*, 'Thy Kingdom come'" (Luke 11:2).

One young man worked at a large secular firm in New York. He felt very intimidated and was sure he was the only believer in the firm. I told him there were probably others there, and to ask God to help him find them. He did, and to his amazement, over the next few weeks he met several other believers who worked at the firm.

Though they came from completely different church traditions, they eagerly began to pray for the Kingdom of God to come in their midst. After a year of praying together, the atmosphere over the business dramatically changed for the better.

Many Christian-owned businesses are setting up prayer rooms in their offices. Some are even opening up these prayer rooms to the public. A doctor in downtown Manhattan, New York has devoted half his office to a public prayer room. His office is right by a subway station and he has prayer meetings every morning before work so people can stop by on their way to work. Similar "Call to the Wall" prayer rooms are starting in downtown Colorado Springs and downtown Wellington, New Zealand, as well as many other places.

Call-to-the-Wall Online

In order to make prayer accessible to everyone, we are making available an online prayer resource center: www.calltothewall.com. Those who are unable to join or start a Call-to-the-Wall gathering can connect to a live prayer feed and pray along.

This site also has a directory of prayer gatherings, HOPE churches, and BizHOPs.